W. Montague Connelly

Political Romanism

A Pocket Manual

W. Montague Connelly

Political Romanism
A Pocket Manual

ISBN/EAN: 9783337020354

Printed in Europe, USA, Canada, Australia, Japan

Cover: Foto ©Suzi / pixelio.de

More available books at **www.hansebooks.com**

POLITICAL ROMANISM

A POCKET MANUAL.

———◆———

BY W. MONTAGUE CONNELLY,

AUTHOR OF THE "FOUR BEASTS."

———◆———

PUBLISHED BY THE

INDEPENDENT PUBLISHING COMPANY.

··· ··· ···

1875.

To Friends of Civil and Religious Liberty.

Believing that, whether you are men of native or foreign birth, whether you are Roman Catholics or Protestants, whether you are capitalists or laborers, the great majority of you sincerely desire the permanence of our Republican institutions, we, on behalf of great principles and important political measures address you. You surely do not desire that free institutions shall be destroyed or subverted even to give political power and pecuniary emolument to the party to which you belong, or the church to which you are attached.

When you see clearly the issues presented, you will prefer the civil and religious liberty of your children and of your children's children, to all shams of party or religion. There is no doubt that you would willingly shed your blood in defence of free institutions, if they were openly or directly assailed, but there is danger that many of you may be led to think it a good thing to crush out the civil and religious liberty of those who do not think as you do. Be assured that this would be the destruction of free Institutions. It would result in the slavery of your children as well as those of others.

If you are friends of civil and religious liberty you should not wish *to force* any one to be or not to be Roman Catholic, Protestant, Infidel or Hebrew. You should have as much respect for the rights of conscience, of person and of property belonging to the man of another political party or religious belief, as you have for your own. The right of every one to secure enjoyment of life, health, reputation, property and opinion, is the foundation of our Republican institutions.

This is why no set of men, the leaders of no political party, the heads of no church organization, have special right to direct or control the government for their advantage, or the promotion of their religion. This is why there should be no union of church and State, no using the law to enforce religious dogmas, no taking of public money to aid church enterprises, no exemption of any private property from bearing its fair share of public burdens.

Holding these opinions, we claim that to maintain free institutions against insidious encroachments, there should be recognition of certain facts.

1st. Civil government is for the regulation of civil affairs in the community according to the will of the majority, so that individual rights may be secure.

2d. No church has the right to assume any functions of the State, or to restrict State authority in the regulation of civil affairs according to the will of the majority.

3d. There should be no alliance of any church with the State. No money collected by taxation for public uses should be given to any church enterprises or political partizans, and no private or church property should be allowed to evade paying its fair share of taxes.

4th. The State should promote the welfare and protect the rights of the whole community by advancing the education needful to make men useful citizens, by establishing relief for the unfortunate, by fairly representing the will of the majority, by securing justice between man and man, and by maintaining civil and religious liberty.

Taking these positions, we ignore and denounce the claim of any church that she has a right to limit the civil power of the State.

We denounce efforts to destroy the Public School System, or to subvert it by making the State support sectarian schools of any denomination.

We denounce all misappropriations of public money to support any church or private enterprises.

We denounce all unjust exemptions of any class of private property belonging to individuals, to churches, or to chartered corporations, from paying its fair share of taxation. It is not Republicanism to tax some men's property and forever exempt from taxation the property of others.

Are not these principles so just, so truly Republican, so needful for the preservation of civil and religious liberty, that you, reader, whether you are Roman Catholic, Protestant, Hebrew or Infidel, and whether you are foreign born or native, can heartily support them.

We ostracise no man for his religious or political opinions, but if we know that a man is seeking to subvert free institutions we will not be willing to place him in power.

If a Roman Catholic is not an enemy of our public school system, if he does not consider it right to prosecute and wage war with heretics, if he condems abstraction of money from the publio treasury for private or sectarian objects, if he is opposed to all union of church and State, and the control of the State by the church, and would not give the Roman Catholic church any greater rights and powers than others, and is an honest and capable man, we have no objection to seeing him in office whether he is native or foreign born.

We war on no man for having been born one place or another.

We war on no man for his religious belief, but we want to be sure that the men who are placed in office are not enemies of free institutions.

WE DEPRECATE THE OSTRACISING OF ANY MAN BECAUSE OF HIS RELIGION.

WE EQUALLY DEPRECATE THE ELECTING OF ANY MAN WHO IS PUT FORWARD BECAUSE HE IS EXPECTED TO FAVOR THE DESIGNS OF A CHURCH ON THE PUBLIC TREASURY, ON CIVIL LIBERTY, ON THE BIBLE, AND ON PUBLIC SCHOOLS.

We believe that at this time the Bishops of the Roman Catholic church are more dangerous to free institutions than the ministers of any other church.

They declare the policy and direct the whole force of the Roman Catholic church.

The Position of Roman Catholic Priests.

There are estimated to be in the United States about 8,500,-000 Catholics controlled by one Cardinal, seven Archbishops, fifty-seven Bishops and 4,500 Priests.

Father Stack, a Roman Catholic priest, says:

"The fact is, the Catholics of America—more than one-fifth of the population—are governed by absolute, irresponsible power, centered in the class of bishops, and wielded by them without regard of any law, civil or ecclesiastical. And so supreme is the arbitrary will of every individual bishop within his diocese that there is no appeal from his fiat. The editor of the New York Freemen's Journal, who is himself a leader of Catholic thought, an able and fearless advocate of the Church, has, with more truth than irony, nicknamed these bishops "the little popes of America." And a distinguished priest, writing in the Freeman (1869,) describes them as "playing the triple role of judge, jury, and hangman." Nor is the description overdrawn. These American bishops accuse and condemn, expel and suspend, excommunicate and punish, without fear of accountability to any law. The 4500 priests of America are reduced to a mere caste, and are so enslaved as to be mere tools in the hands of the bishops. The priests have no sort of representation; they have no voice in synod; none in the election or nomination of their masters, the bishops. Instead of holding their office for life, as the law of the church guarantees, they are liable to be deprived of their rank and emoluments, and to be cast friendless upon the world by the caprice of the bishop's will. Their honor, their reputation, their livelihood, are at the mercy of the bishop. I might say their very life is at his mercy; for if you deprive men of the means of living—and the avocation of a clergyman is the only one for which most of them are qualified—do you not virtually deprive them of life? But has the priest no remedy in the Church? He has, and he has not. He has, *de jure*; and he has not *de facto*. The law of the Church provides for an ecclesiastical tribunal to try and adjudicate in all differences between priests and bishops. But the bishop interposes his *non placet*, and will not allow any such thing as an eccleslastical tribunal in America. What, then, is left for the priest but to have recourse to civil law to enforce his *rights of contract* with the Church? And yet if he so falls back on his citizenship, he is likely to get excommunicated for his pains. The priests are slaves, and, at the same time, the instruments of the enslaving power. They are the men who move among the people, and talk to them and execute among them the orders of the bishops. There is not a Catholic paper in America that can afford to strike out, with any hope of success, independently of the bishops. No Catholic dares to sue a bishop except at the peril of his soul's salvation, and thus Catholics are practically debarred, as far as bishops are concerned, from enjoying the common rights of citizenship. The law of the land might as well be blotted out when there is question among Catholics of power of bishops.''

WHAT THE ALL POWERFUL BISHOPS SWEAR TO DO.

The oath that must be taken by all Roman Catholic Bishops when they receive the pallium, is given in the Pontifical Romanum in the Antwerp, Paris and Roman Editions, and it contains in Latin the obligation: "HERETICS, SCHISMATICS, AND REBELS TO THE SAID LORD (THE POPE) OR HIS AFORESAID SUCCESSORS, I WILL TO THE UTTERMOST OF MY POWER, PROSECUTE AND WAGE WAR WITH, SO HELP ME GOD AND THOSE HOLY GOSPELS OF GOD.''

Under the authority of Pope Clement 8th, and Pope Urban 8th, and with Catelanos' notes, it is determined that this Pontifical oath "shall not at any time be changed in whole or in part, and nothing shall be added to it and nothing subtracted from it." The Pontificale further says: "when the Pallium is sent from the Apostolic See, the Pontiff to whom the delivery of it is committed, meets with the elected in his own church or in some church of his diocese on a fixed day. When the pallium is spread on the altar, covered with the silk in which it was carried, mass being finished, the Pontiff sitting on a gold stool recites the *oath of fidelity* from the Archbishop elect in the name of the Apostolic See, the elect kneeling before him in his pontificals and without gloves.''

How comes it that this Bishop's and Archbishop's oath is never published in Roman Catholic papers, when they give ornate and minute descriptions of such ceremonials. Is there a conciousness that such an oath is against the spirit of toleration and religious liberty?

THE CLAIM OF THE R. C. CHURCH.

The Roman church claims that she has from God the right to define and thus limit the authority of any state or nation in which she exists. She always has and does now oppose the right of the state to subject her priests to the same civil duties as are required of other men. She always has and does now oppose the right of the state to allow liberty of Speech or the Press. She always has and does now oppose the right of the State to issue a writ of Habeas Corpus to see whether any one is held in ecclesiastical imprisonment contrary to his or her own will.

WHAT THE PRESENT POPE HAS DONE.

The present Pope has declared void laws of Spain, Piedmont, Austria, New Grenada, Mexico and Sardinia, that gave toleration to other than the Roman Religion, and established freedom of the press and religious worship. Last year the Pope declared that Prussian subjects should not obey the laws passed by the Prussian Legislature, in relation to schools supported by the State. The Pope has very recently demanded of King Alphonso that the Roman church shall be placed in Spain as it was before the revolution, that is : all other public worship forbidden, and Protestant churches and cemeteries disallowed.

If Rome could, she would demand in this country, what she demands in Spain. It is for that end that she is using all the influence she can command.

POWER OF ROME.

"There must be less petty jealousies amongst us; nationalities must be made subordinate to religion, and we must learn that *we are Catholics first and citizens next.* Catholicity does not bring us in conflict with the State, yet it teaches that God is above man, and *the Church above the State."—Bishop Gilmer,* (*Roman Catholic.*)

" This doctrine is the legitimate and logical result of the Dogma of Infallibility, and makes the Church identical with God, and its authority paramount with His. It is but one step from this position to the Inquisition. All that is wanting is *power to compel comformity,* for Romanism, so expressed, to crush civil and religious liberty.—*Cleaveland Leader.*

" The ecclesiastical power is superior to the civil, and defines the limit of one and the other."—*M. Capel,* (*Great Roman Catholic authority.*)

" Whenever any Law of man, whether relating to spiritual or temporal affairs, conflicts with any Law of God, as it is interpreted to the world by the infallible Pope of Rome, it is to be disobeyed and the latter is to be substituted for it."— *Western Catholic.*

" If the liberties of the American people are ever destroyed, they will fall by the hands of the Romish clergy.—*Lafayette.*

Give the Roman Catholic Church the power, and she would be untrue to her whole history, untrue to the utterances of the great body of her clergy, untrue to the threats of her church papers, untrue to her convictions, untrue to the oaths of her Bishops, if she did not persecute and wage war on heretics, did not seek to control or break down what she calls the Godless public schools, did not abolish the free reading of the Bible and toleration of all religions. She has never yet had the power in Maryland to do so. It may be said that Methodists, Baptists and Presbyterians would do the same if *they* had the power. We are not considering now what other sects MIGHT do, but what the Roman Catholic Church has done, is doing and swears to do. Certainly no other Church claims the right to declare the *limit* of the power of the State. In no other Church do Bishops swear to oppose free toleration of other religions.

Roman Catholics are as much interested as any other citizens in knowing whether under the guidance of Bishops and Jesuits, the Church they love is the friend or foe of religious liberty.

The heads of the Roman Church are now laboring to consolidate its different parts. This is the purpose that influences the dedications to the Sacred Heart of Jesus, the Catholic Temperance unions, &c., &c.

ROMANISM JUSTIFIES THE ABSTRACTION OF PUBLIC MONEY FOR HER USE.

The Romanist Church always urges and applauds the abstraction of public money from the public treasury and giving it to aid her enterprises. No Romanist paper, Priest, Bishop, Archbishop or Cardinal has ever uttered one word of condemnation of Tweed, Connolly, Sweeny, and the other New York ring thieves, for having stolen from the public treasury and given to Romish Church enterprises in three years, $1,915,456 92 of the people's money, nor one word of condemnation of the same thieves having given, in the same three years, $3,500,000 worth of public property to the same Romish enterprises.

When the Roman Catholic Church in New York got in 1869 $510,071 82, in 1870 $464,681 05, in 1871 $121,625 64 of the money that belonged to the public, and that the donors had no right to give to the Church, the Methodist Church got in the whole three years only $7,270 95, the Baptists only $5,325 83 altogether, the Presbyterians only $13,960 52 altogether, the German Evangelicals only $3,691 16 altogether, the Reformed Dutch only $22,220 06 altogether, and the Episcopalians only $56,956 74 altogether.

It may be said that it was luck—that the other churches took all they could get. Even that would not make the abstraction right or the division fair, but the fact is that from the first many persons and sectarian papers of the Methodist, Baptist and other Churches, were opposed to taking such illegal donations, and so strong was this feeling that in 1871 and afterwards the Presbyterians, Baptists, Methodists, Reformed Dutch, and German Evangelical Churches in New York, neither asked nor would receive such donations, which in 1871 alone amounted to $421,625 64 to the Roman Catholic Church. Everywhere in all large cities the Roman Catholic Church has desired and urged the donation to her of such abstractions. Her Archbishops, Bishops and Priests have petitioned for such union of Church and State, such abstractions of public money.

The Romanist Church bitterly denounces any public man who opposes such misuse of money collected by taxation for public uses. It is no proscription of Roman Catholics to oppose this constant universal policy and practice of the Roman Catholic Church.

While the Episcopalians, Reformed Dutch, German Evangelicals, Baptists and Methodists, who pay three fourths of all the taxes in New York, only had donations of public money amounting to $357,774 47 in three years, the Roman Catholic Church, whose people do not pay one-third of the taxes, was presented with $1,915,456 92 out of the public treasury, and had $3,500,- 000 of public property given to it also.

When Archbishop Bayley was welcomed here, a leading politician boasted that "no Roman Catholic institution asking money from the city treasury had ever been refused."

The *Western Catholic* denounces those who favor taxing ecclesiastical property in common with all other private property, as "knaves" "social pests," "immoral and disorganizing drones," as "guilty of mendacious pretences" and "hypocritical greed," and as "actuated by personal greed and personal revenge," "undertaking to reform even the Creator himself."

The American doctrine is that those who hold office in the State or city have the right to pay just claims on the State or city, but have no right to donate public money to any person or institution when there is no legal claim.

The old south church property in Boston was donated for religious purposes over a hundred years ago, when it was worth $6,000. The lot is worth now at least $500,000. It has never paid taxes since its donation, and as the church was burned down, the congregation wanted the legislature to give permission for them to sell the lot, pocket the money, and build a church somewhere else. Mr. Josiah Phillip Quincy, a leader of the church taxation movement, claims that the lot must be used for religious purposes, or the back taxes must be paid, or the proceeds of the sale paid over to the public treasury before the church owners can give a title.

The *National Baptist* says:—The whole matter is settled when you have answered two questions. 1st. Has civil society a right to give the public money to a religious or ecclesiastical body, to a missionary society, a tract society or a church? According to the theory of all the state-church governments, civil society has this right. Is this the American view?

The burden of impartial taxation should fall indiscriminately on all denominations, among which the Methodists have nine millions more, and the Presbyterians but thirteen millions less than the sixty-one millions of Catholic property.

A Committee of the Illinois Conference of the M. E. Church has reported in favor of the taxation of church property. They argue in their report that the Constitution forbids the State to aid any religious denomination, and that laws which exempt $382,000,000 worth of church property from taxation violates the letter and spirit of the Constitution. The committee add that the taxation of church property would be favorable to the interest of religion by showing that the separation between the Church and the State is complete.

The assessors of the District of Columbia have valued the lots and church property belonging to the various denominations as follows: Washington, $1,425,794; Georgetown, $115,955; and county, $48,295, the whole being $1,590,744. This is the basis on which they purpose to tax them, contrary to previous usage.

The Roman Catholic institution, the St. Mary's Industrial School, has employed a Protestant lawyer to enable her to get hold of the public money appropriated by the City Council and stopped by injunction.

Romanism would banish the Bible.

Pope Gregory VII condemned the general freedom allowed to read the Bible in the vulgar tongue.

Pope Innocent declared the Bible too profound for the common people, and quoted the text "If so be that a beast touch the Mountain it shall be stoned or thurst through with a dart."

Pope Clement II, in a Bull pronounced it a false, scandalous, pernicious, blasphemous error to hold that all may read the Holy Scriptures.

Pope Benedict XIV opposed a translation of the Bible.

Pope Leo XII issued an Encyclical against Bible societies.

Pope Pius VII issued a Bull forbidding the circulation of the Scriptures.

Pope Pius IX, in 1846, anathematized "those very crafty and deceitful societies called Bible societies, which thrust the Bible into the hands of inexperienced youth."

Archbishop Ximenes said, "It is utterly wrong to circulate the scriptures in the vulgar tongue."

16

Cardinal Hosius said, "To give the Bible to the laity is to cast pearls before swine. Bible translations have done harm. I would not have any."

The council of Toulouse (1229) declared "That the laity must not possess the books of the Old and New Testament."

The council of Terracona (1233) declared that any one priest or layman who had a translation of the Bible and did not in eight days give it up to be burnt should be esteemed a heretic.

The Synod of Oxford (1406) denounced having the Bible in English.

ROMANISM AND PUBLIC SCHOOLS.

The Roman church is the foe of public free schools, unless she can control them for her own purposes.

There are Roman Catholics who are the friends of public schools, and there are others who have no special opposition to public schools, but prefer to have their children under the priests in the church schools, and would like to lessen their taxes for education. But the Church as a church, controlled by the bishops and Jesuits, is opposed to all schools not controlled by the priests.

Rome has claimed that she only had the right to educate and to marry, and she has opposed as far as she could civil marriages and public schools.—*Intelligencer.*

It is not unreasonable to suppose that *the Catholic clergy are intent on incorporating their schools with the public schools, where this can be done with safety to their own influence.* But this scheme is not likely to succeed any better than the other.— *New York Times.*

Rome denounces all schools not controlled by priests.

Some Roman Catholics may not be foes of public or Protestant schools, but the Roman Catholic church is, and its sentiment is fairly expressed by the following : "I would as soon administer the sacraments to a dog as to Catholics who send their children to the public schools."—*Father Walker.*

" What Father Walker says is only what has been said by the bishops all over the world, over and over again in their pastorals, and we heartily endorse it."—*New York Tablet.*

"When I see them drag from me the children, the poor little children, and give them an Infidel education, it breaks my heart.—*Pope Pius IX.*

"When Catholic parents understand that they cannot have absolution in the confessionals while they let their children go to Godless or to Protestant schools, they will soon find a remedy. —*Freeman's Journal.*

The schoolmasters of Italy, in a congress which they recently held at Bologna, passed a resolution adverse to religious instruction in public schools. It asserts " the incompetency of the State to impart instruction in dogmatic religion in public elementary schools, and would leave to the municipalities, if request be made by families, the faculty of regulating such instruction in the mode which they may consider the most opportune."

The *Catholic Telegraph*, of Cincinnati, says: "The 47th and 48th articles of the Syllabus have authoritatively settled for all time that the exclusion of religious instruction, [that is, not of other religions but of Romanism,] is a damnable error which Catholics cannot approve without a denial of faith and commission of sin."

Last year fifty-one Roman Catholic bishops and archbishops sent to the French Assembly a protest against establishing a public school system, declaring that a public secular education would breed more mischiefs to France than all the disasters of the war.

"The public schools have produced nothing but a Godless generation of thieves and blackguards."—*Father Schauer.*

Last year Father Konings wrote a pamphlet in which he held that in exceptional cases it might be right to grant absolution to parents who send their children to the Godless public schools, whereupon the *Freeman's Journal* said : " We can tell Father Konings that it is far better for the children of Catholics to run in the streets under the even occasional watch of their parents than to send them to these acknowledged nests of all abominations, the Godless public schools."

The Catholic members of the New Brunswick House of Assembly, headed by Mr. Burns, had a conference with the Government in reference to making such modifications of the School Act as shall make it acceptable to the Catholics of the Province. It is rumored that the propositions put forward refer, first to the attendance at school of Catholic children in populous districts ; to the mode of licensing the Christian Brothers and Sisters of Charity on certain tests ; to the substitution for objectionable books in history and reading of others approved by the Board, and to the allowance of religious instruction after school hours.

The Roman Catholic church holds that all schools should be broken up unless a Roman Catholic education is given in them. She never has recognized the right of heresy to exist. She claims that she has the right from God to determine how far her own authority extends. She always denies the right of the State to limit her authority.

Sincere Roman Catholics.

The more sincere a Roman Catholic is, the greater will be his zeal in sustaining his church if he sympathizes with her in her hatred of all but Romanist schools as Godless Formerly the Roman Catholic church denied that the State had a right to levy a school tax. She claimed that the State had no right to establish or support schools since education belonged to the church. Recently in New York and other States, the Roman Catholic church demands that the State shall support her schools while the priests control them. To this it is objected that the State has no right to support any church or private schools, and that attempting to support all sectarian schoo's would break up the whole public school system and consign millions of children to ignorance.

Reading the Bible.

The question of reading the Protestant Bible in schools is not the issue. The reading of any Bible is denounced by the Roman Catholic church. Pope Gregory 7th condemned the general freedom allowed of reading the Bible in the vulgar tongue. Pope Innocent 3d declared that the common people should not be allowed to read the Scriptures. Pope Clement 11th declared it a "false, scandalous, pernicious, blasphemous error, to hold that all may read the Holy Scriptures." Pope Benedict 14th opposed a translation of the Bible into Persian. Pope Pius 7th, in a Bull, forbade the circulation of the Scriptures. The council of Trent declared that the forgiveness of sins should be withheld from any man who "shall dare to have a Bible in the vulgar tongue" without a license from his ecclesiastical superiors. Many similar declarations of Roman

Catholic authorities might be given. The Roman Catholic church is hostile to the general reading of any version of the Bible, but if no Bible was used in the public schools the Roman Catholic church would still declare them Godless, and would seek to control or break them down. The more a Roman Catholic is in sympathy with his church, the stronger will be his wish to break down the public schools. He may be a sincere, moral, honest man, but his church is the enemy of Bible reading, of public schools, of toleration of other religions.

Archbishop Bayley, in his pastoral letter of February 6th, 1875, laments the good old times before the French revolution, when "to have sent a child to a school were religious teachings were excluded, would have been regarded as virtual apostacy, when mixed marriages were almost unknown, and when there was not such license as is now granted to the young in the company they kept, the books and newspapers they read, and the places of amusement they visited, and when the standard of duty and practice was higher than at present, and he declares "we must return to the old path."

Rochester, New York, has by a vote of twelve to four in its Board of education, determined that all religious exercises of any nature shall be prohibited in the public schools. This is the American idea of secular education by the State, not claiming that such education is all that children need, but taking the position that it is all that the State can furnish at the public expense.—*New York Times.*

The Right of All to Habeas Corpus.

In nearly all countries of the World it is being discovered that confinement in an Ecclesiastical prison should not deprive any one of civil rights to habeas corpus, and damages for enforced imprisonment, and this principle will, says the Methodist, compel the supervision of all monastic institutions in this country. It says :

"Monastic institutions in France exist on two conditions, authorized or incorporated, and unauthorized or unincorporated. Authorization is not given until inquiries are made as to the objects and utility of the proposed religious house. Each authorized monastic establishment is subject to the supervision of the State. Vows are permitted, but not for a longer term than five years. Any member who wishes to leave can do so ; the taking of vows does not destroy civil rights, as was once held by the church. Unless authorized by the government in France, religious communities cannot accept gifts, or grants of real estate. The Government also reserves to itself the right to withdraw authorization which it has given. It is estimated that there are 2,000 houses of men, containing 20,000 persons under vows, one-fourth of whom are devoted to a life of contemplation. The majority of these organizations are not authorized by the State. About 100,000 women in France belong to religious orders; most of them are engaged actively in works of charity. The French government is disposed to be tolerant in its supervision of monastic orders, and yet does keep them under its observation. In Portugal monasteries have been abolished ; in Sweden and Norway they are not tolerated! The Spanish Cortes, in 1868, suppressed the monasteries, but in 1872 they were sanctioned again. Since 1864, in Russia, the entry into monastic orders and the admission of novices cannot take place without the consent of the local civil authorities. In Autria recent legislation has greatly limited the independence which monastic institutions formerly enjoyed. In Switzerland they have been put under strict surveillan e, and in some cantons suppressed.

The Romanist Church denying civil and religious liberty, claims that the State shall not dare to investigate whether there are Roman Catholic Prisons in which unwilling victims are confined. It is ready to war against any writ of Habeas Corpus to ascertain whether a poor monk or nun is confined or punished illegally and against their own consent.

The foregoing facts show that Rome aims to control the State so that she may restrict civil and religious liberty, may have her schools supported by the State, and may have abstractions of money from the public treasury for her advantage. To oppose her in these things is not ostracising any man on account of his religion. She aims to put men in office to carry out her designs. The friends of free institutions should see that her tools are not put where they can imperil civil and religious liberty, or plunder the public or aid Rome in evading just public burdens. We do not oppose Romanism politically except when it attempts to tear down or undermine the temple of liberty.

OTHER WRONGS.

Rome is not the only raider on public treasuries. There is altogether in Baltimore over sixty million dollars worth of property that unjustly escapes paying its fair share of taxes. The taxes collected from it should amount at least to six or eight hundred thousand dollars a year. That amount is unjustly taken every year from other property owners. It is an unjust thing that the Baltimore and Ohio Railroad Company pays no taxes on the Camden street property, nor on any other, and will pay none on the palace it is about to erect on the corner of Calvert and Baltimore streets.

Sworn statements of officers of eight city railroads in New York in 1874, showed that public property worth more than $10,000,000 has been given away to private corporations by the city and State. Is there no mode of recovery or redress or punishment?

There is in New York City between $275,000,000 and $320,-000,000 of property that fraudulently evades taxation. Altogether 826 pieces of property in 1873 escaped taxation, and their estimated value was $275,000,000.

In 1850 the church property in the United States exempt from taxation was worth $87,328,801 ; in 1860 it was $171,397,932 ; in 1870 it was $344,483,481, and is now over $600,000,000.

Of the magistrates in Baltimore who have the fattest places, two-thirds are Roman Catholics. This is a larger proportion than seems fair.

MISCELLANEOUS MATTERS.

Liberty of conscience in all the American plantations was established by the English House of Commons in 1645, the year in which King Charles was defeated at Naseby, and in accordance with that establishment of liberty of conscience, Maryland, of which the government was 16 Protestants and 8 Catholics, in 1649 passed its act of toleration to all avowed Christians.

Before A. D. 306, heresy was subject to cursing and excommunication, after A. D. 306, it was made punishable by death.

The first Inquisitors were appointed by Theodosius, in A. D. 382. The first penal code against heretics was in A. D. 529, when Justinian decreed that the canons of previous general

Synods should be laws. About A. D. 800, courts were established to sustain the power of western Bishops and punish those who offended them.

Pope Innocent 3d, who excommunicated King John of England, framed rules for the Inquisitional missions that he sent out. Pope Gregory 9th, in A. D. 1233, established these rules and appointed the Dominicans to enforce them. New instructions to inquisitors were promulgated in 1484, and 1561.

Lloriente states that in 236 years, the Roman Catholic Inquisition put 32,000 persons to death in Spain alone, and subjected 291,000 to other punishments. It was finally abolished in Spain in 1820 when the Spanish revolution began.

The Council of Chalcidon, A. D. 451, (canon 15) made it unlawful for readers or singers to marry a woman of heterodox opinions.

The Conncil of Laodicia, (canon 31) said "no son or daughter should marry a heretic."

The Council of Orleans, A. D. 532, prohibited marriages between Jews and Christians.

The 4th Conncil of Toledo ordered separation, if the Jews wonld not join the Christian faith.

The Council of Neo Caesarea, A. D. 315, (7 canon) declared a presbyter must not be the groom at the wedding of a person marrying a second time.

"The Romanism of the day in a measure repays its obligation by making its censure of evils sincere, no doubt, but only light and rare in comparison with the anathemas which it bestows upon liberty and its guarantees, most of all when any tendency to claim them is detected within its own precinct."
W. E. Gladstone.

The Catholic Review estimates that from 1761 to 1872 the Pope got from Peter's Pence $80,000,000.

In A. D. 330 the special powers and privileges of christian Bishops were recognized and established by the Roman Emperor; and under the Lombard and Norman Kings the Clergy in the seventh and eighth centuries (between A. D. 600 and A. D. 700,) gained much temporal power.

When James Russell Lowell in Italy asked a solicitor for aid—"why do you apply to a heretic,"—the reply was "your money is perfectly orthodox."

The popes that have issued Bulls against Freemasons and other secret societies have been Clement XII, in 1730, Benedict XIV, in 1751, Leo XII, in 1806, Pius VII, in 1811, and Pius IX, in 1865.

In different ages Rome has made beliefs *obligatory* that previously were not so. Thus monkery was established A. D. 380, Mass A. D. 391, Auricular Confession A. D. 425, Purgatory A. D. 593, Invocation of Virgin Mary A. D. 715, Transubstantiation A. D. 910, Celibacy of priests A. D. 1010, Indulgences A. D. 1014, Tiara A. D. 1048, Dispensations A. D. 1200, Inquisition A. D. 1200, Seven Sacraments A. D. 1439, Immaculate Conception A. D. 1860, Papal infallibility A. D. 1870.

Pius IX receives higher wages than any other sovereign of Europe. His average monthly income is $2,000,000.—*Cincinnati Commercial.*

The Pope wears out during the year six white silk capuchins, which his Holiness chiefly spoils by taking snuff; these cost Pius IX $80 a piece. His slippers, made of red cloth, embroidered in gold, cost from $25 to $30 a pair, and half a dozen pairs are used during the year, while the Pope in winter wears silk stockings over cotton ones, and in summer a mixture of silk and thread, for both of which he pay $5 a pair. His Holiness' red mantle is worth $160. His cast-off garments are always burnt, no other use being thought sufficiently honorable for the clothes which have been worn by the vicar of heaven.—*Free Press.*

"The Holy Catholic religion reigns triumphant in Mexico, and the Free Masons are correspondingly depressed and discouraged. Late files of Mexican news papers bring information that a company of pious bandits have sacked and burned the Village of Lancitaro, the State of Guererro. They made the attack, shouting "Viva la Religion!" The same battle-cry, with the additional fervid invocation, "Death to Masons!" has been raised in Sinaloa.—*Chicago Tribune.*

There are in this Country 7 different orders of monks or friars, 12 of Nuns, 8 different Institutions, such as Jesuits and Redemptorists, 12 congregations of Priests and Brothers, and 30 Sisterhoods.

Throughout the world in 1874 there were 6 Cardinal Bishops, 37 Cardinal Priests, and 7 Cardinal Deacons. Total 50.

The College of Cardinals when complete, has 70 members. Of the fifty present Cardinals, 30 are Italians, 7 Spanish, 6 French, 3 German. To this time from A. D. 752, when the Papal Temporal Power was fully recognized, there has been 163 Popes, of whom 137 were Italians.

Cardinal Cullen in a recent pastoral, reminded Catholics that the censures of the Church had been repeatedly pronounced against Secret Societies.

An old soldier in Sicily gave his wife a silk dress. His wife died and was buried in the dress. Some weeks after the old soldier saw this dress on a woman in the country, and, making inquiry, was told she had purchased it from the Capuchin monks, who had the custody of the village cemetery. He reported the case to the police, who investigated, and made the discovery that a regular trade was carried on in effects taken from dead bodies. There was even a trade in hair.

" We said the legislature should not grant divorces, but the courts. The *Catholic Standard* thereupon charges that we yield the free-lovers' premises, and says that neither courts nor legislatures have any right to grant divorces. Well, supposing there is scriptural ground for divorce; who shall grant it, if not some legal authority which can settle alimony? Shall the priest, with appeal to the bishop? Who shall be the judge of fact?"—*Episcopal Register*.

The title Pope was at one time given to all Bishops. It was first adopted by Hygineus in A. D. 139. Phocas, Emperor of the East, in 606 confined the title to the prelates of Rome. In the 708 the kissing of the Pope's toe began. In 1773 kissing the Pope's toe was abolished.

Pope Adrian I. in 780 caused money to be coined in his name. The first Pope who kept an army was Leo IX., in A. D. 1054. Appeals from the decisions of English tribunals to the Pope began in A. D. 1154. Gregory VII. obliged the Emperor of Germany to stand three days in the depth of winter barefooted, at the gate of the Castle of Canossa, to implore his pardon. King Henry II. of England held the stirrup for Pope Alexander III. to mount his horse in A. D. 1161. In 1191 Pope Celestine III., to show his prerogative of making and un-making kings, kicked the crown off the head of the Emperor Henry VI., who was kneeling before him.

If it is alleged that the quotatians given in this little book do not fairly present Roman Catholic sentiment, let the objector cite any contrary opinions advanced by Roman Catholic Bishops, newspapers, or other Roman Catholic authorities.

In September, 1875, *there are to be nine* new Cardinals of the Romish Church created. It is said that they will be Antica, Pacsa, Ricci, Nina, Giannelli, Serafini, Virelleschi, Simeoni, Randi and Canonico Andisio. This will increase the power of the Jesuits.

The clerical (R. C.) party in France has just gained a great victory in its struggle for the control of education. The power lost by the priests in 1793 was out of their hands almost wholly until 1848, when through the Compte de Falloux they gained once more a foothold, and now under the Bishop of Orleans they have made a further advance. There has been such a cry, led on by Bishop Dupanloup, of the impiety of the instructions given by the professors of the State, that now the Roman Catholic Church is to be allowed to establish free universities, to which bequests can be made, and then the influence of the clergy over death-bed penitents will bring a rich harvest. Heretofore such bequests have not been allowed in France.

The Bavarian Bishops last year protested against the law recognizing civil marriages.

"In the city of Brooklyn $338,600 of taxes that should come every year from church corporations, which are largely composed of rich men, is made up by taxing poor men, widows and others, more than their fair proportion."

ROME COMTEMPLATES POLITICAL ACTION.

"An immense preponderance of electoral power is in the hands of the Catholics of this city, so that their united action would secure the success of any party or any question on behalf of which it should be secured."—*N. Y. Tablet, a Roman Catholic Paper.*

When pressing the demands of the R. C. Church on the Board of Education in New York, Father Preston said : "If the compromise was not effected, he (Father Preston) thought it not at all unlikely that the Roman Catholics would organize, so as to decide the question IN THEIR FAVOR AT THE POLLS." The threat made in New York is being carried out. She already controls the Democratic Party, she fills the offices, she directs State and Municipal Legislation, she has a foothold in the School Board. Her movements are seen in New York, Michigan, Ohio, Missouri, Maryland and other States.

"The saying is attributed to Lafayette : ' If ever the liberties of the United States be destroyed it will be by Roman priests.' I deny this ; and I offer in place of it the truer saying : ' If ever the liberties of the United States be destroyed it will be by *Roman Bishops*.' Let the blame rest where it belongs."—*Father Stack*, (*R. C.*)

"I am no prophet, and I am not anxious to hazard a prophesy, but I am bold to say that I anticipate contention and angry strife from the relation of the Catholic Church under the sway of the Bishops to the American Republic."—*Father Stack*, (*R. C.*)

"The Power of the Roman Catholic Bishops of America is a tyranny within the Church and *a standing danger to the liberties of the country*."—*Father Stack*, (*R. C.*)

"In America many priests now silent for fear of the Mitre, only await the opportunity to advocate common schools and all the institutions of the Republic."—*Father Stack*, (*R. C.*)

We deny that any form of sectarian religion should be aided by the State or have its dogmas taught in national work-shops or public schools. This is not saying that religion should not be taught at all anywhere. The political Romanist declares that no religion which he considers heretical should be taught in any public school, but he insists that the State should either allow the teaching of Romanism in the public schools, or support Roman Catholic schools and let the Roman Church control them.

THE COURT HOUSE RING.

It is a notorious fact in this City of Baltimore, that what is called the Court House Ring dictates all democratic nominations. Who are these all powerful rulers of Baltimore Democracy ?

Don't everybody know they are I. Freeman Rasin, (Roman Catholic,) Clerk of the Court of Common Pleas; Wm. McKewen, (Roman Catholic,) Clerk of the Criminal Court; A. Albert, (Roman Catholic,) Sheriff, and probably Tax Collector; O. Keilholtz, (Roman Catholic,) President of the First Branch ; Mr. Bannon, through whom the the House of Correction property was bought; A. Leo Knott, (Roman Catholic,) State's Attorney, who is to be re-elected ; Dr. Slater, a sporting man, and a few others of less prominence. These are the rulers of the Democratic party in Baltimore. There are clever gentlemen those in office comparing favorably with any of their predecessors. They are courteous, and perhaps really think it would be to the advantage of the country to have the ideas of the Roman Catholic Church in relation to the Bible, the public schools, the rights of the State and toleration prevail.

No great lawyer, no leading merchant, no prominent business man, nor indeed all the great lawyers, leading merchants and prominent business men in Baltimore have as much influence in the securing of places and spoils, or in directing Democratic party movements, as any one of the members of the ring.

Through these men Rome now hopes to have a Governor elected who will not keep her hands out of the public treasury, nor interfere with her undermining of the public schools.

Rome is now hoping to elect a City Council that will put in the School Board men favorable to her designs. When recently an intense Romanist wished to be Superintendent of Public Instruction, he got 8 votes, and there were only 11 against him.

Don't be scared at the howls of the ring and their pack that you are proscriptive because you will only trust in office men whom you know to be friends of free institutions, and unhesitating opponents of all attempts to break down the public schools or to restrict freedom of speech and the press and religious toleration. It is not proscriptive to refuse to vote for men who even honestly support harmful conspiracies, or who are not outspoken friends of entire religious toleration and free institutions.

The direct abstractions from our City Treasury have not been large heretofore. They have been to Roman Catholic enterprises much larger than to those of any other sect. Thus, the Roman Catholic ones in 1872, $6,500; 1873, $9,550; 1874, $6,500, and this year it will be over $17,000. Are there not many citizens of this country who are Catholics first and Americans afterwards?

The Roman Catholic Church expects to have a majority in the City Council that is about to be elected. From the men put forward the indications are that the next Council may not be composed of as good material as the present. It is conceded that some of the present members who vote as the Roman Catholic Church desires are otherwise honest men and conscientious. In the next Council it is possible there will not be a single voice raised against sectarian appropriations. The Council that is to be elected will select the School Commissioners ; Rome then may control the very institutions that she seeks to break down.

The managers of the democratic party in Baltimore, are not conscientious Roman Catholics! They care only for spoils. They would betray the Church of Rome if they found it a political advantage. To win they are for "Carroll and Papal Aggressions," or for their man Groome, if he is more likely to win.

At the last session of the State Legislature, there was a feeling that expenditures to Sectarian Institutions were becoming too excessive, and there was an agreement to stop them. Several Protestant appropriations were killed and there was no complaint. When a Catholic donation was proposed, Barney Harig a Catholic, and Dr. Chaisty, had the manliness to adhere to their agreement and vote against such abstractions, and for doing so they were subject to priestly denunciations and to a storm of abuse, slander and denunciations. They were denounced from the altar and to be reelected they have had to make their peace with Rome.

When recently over a hundred Presbyterian, Methodist and other ministers respectfully called the attention of the City Council to the fact, that any giving of public money to any but public uses, any giving to aid any church in its enterprises, was dangerous and illegal, there was a powerful R. C. influence brought to bear to oppose it. In the Second Branch three members, Messrs Kirk, Loney and Hogg dared to speak against all appropriations, *not for public uses*. They were against all private and sectarian appropriations. Those favoring R. C. appropriations declared that all appropriations, even to *public* institutions, must be struck out if the R. C. appropriations were. This Mr. Murray also opposed by his vote. Messrs. Loney,

Hogg and Kirk were voted down. When the bill went into the First Branch, not one member dared to oppose sectarian appropriations, though every speaker admitted they were contrary to the letter of the Law and hence illegal. Every member knew that to speak against sectarian donations, was to face political death. Mr. Heuisler knew that if he did not justify the appropriations to his church, and assail Messrs. Hogg, Loney and Kirk as moral cowards, who had wilted before the ministers, he would certainly not go back to the Council.

Mr. Stewart, though a nominal protestant, thought it necessary to make a gross attack on the ministers. Every member of the First Branch who was present voted for sectarian appropriations.

JESUITS.

The Jesuits now rule the Roman Catholic Church. They are its backbone. One of their order, or one in whom it has confidence, will be the next Pope. Only that order can now lead in the great struggle of Romanism to govern the world. The Jesuits more heartily than any other of the Romanist orders, has supported the doctrine of the infallibility of the Pope, and one of its four vows is *implicit submission to the Holy See.*

Ignatius Loyola laid the foundation of this order at Paris in 1534. The institution of the Society of Jesus was confirmed by a Bull of Pope Paul III in 1540, but the number of members was restricted to sixty. This restriction was taken off in 1543. Great privileges were granted to the order by Popes Julius III, Pius V, and Gregory XIII.

In France the Society of Jesus was condemned by the Sorbonne in 1554, expelled in 1594, readmitted 1604, and expelled and its property confiscated in 1764, then expelled in 1831 and 1845. In England it was expelled in 1579, 1581, 1586, 1692 and 1829.

It was expelled from Venice in 1607 ; from Holland in 1708 : from Portugal in 1759 and 1834 ; from Spain in 1767, 1820 and 1835 ; from Belgium in 1818 ; from Russia in 1820 ; from Sardinia and Austria in 1848, and from Italy and Sicily in 1860. If it had not been everywhere found peculiarly dangerous and harmful, it would scarcely have found more opposition everywhere than other Roman Catholic orders, as the Dominicans, Franciscans, Trappists, &c., &c.

In 1769 Pope Clement XIV suppressed the Jesuits as a dangerous order, but Pope Pius VI restored them in 1814.

"The banishment of the Jesuits from Germany has appealed to the Catholic hospitality of other parts of the world, and the Monastery at Quincy, Illinois, has generously tendered a refuge and home to two hundred of the expatriated priests. It is contemplated to convert Quincy into the headquarters of the Order in the United States.—*N. Y. World*.

The Jesuits have sixteen colleges distinctively their own in the United States, and their emissaries are in chairs of instruction in many institutions not suspected of being under their control. The number of actual sworn members of the order in the United States and Canada in 1874 was 1,062, of whom 251 were in the missions of New York and Canada, —*Methodist Advocate*.

WHAT JESUITS WANT.

"The teacher of teachers is the church itself."—*Bishop Mc-Quaid*.

35

This Bishop in his speech in Rochester, N. Y., May, 1875, said he proposed to carry "the question of the public schools to the ballot-box."

"Protestantism of every form has not, and never can have, any right where Catholicity has triumphed; and therefore we lose the breath we expend in declaiming against bigotry and intolerance, and in favor of religious liberty, or the right of any man to be of any religion as best pleases him."—*Catholic Review*.

The Archbishop of St. Louis said: "If the Catholics ever gain—which they assuredly will—an immense numerical majority, religious freedom in this country will be at an end."

"Religious liberty is merely endured until the opposite can be carried into effect without peril to the Catholic world."— *Bishop O' Conner*.

"The Catholic Church numbers one-third the American population, and if its membership shall increase for the next thirty years as it has for the thirty years past, in 1900 Rome will have a majority, and be bound to take this country and keep it.— There is, ere long, to be a State religion in this country, and that State religion is to be Roman Catholic."—*Father Hecker*.

The *Civila Cattolica*, the organ of the Jesuits in Rome, has again and again proclaimed that "the battle against Protestantism must be opened along the whole line, and the war caaried on until it lies powerless."

FRATERNITIES.

Fraternities are of different sorts, each of which has, perhaps, special merits and defects. They are:

1. Fraternal and incidentally beneficial, as Masons, &c.

2. Mutual and beneficial, as Odd Fellows, &c.

3. Trade, as of carpenters, coopers, &c., for the benefit of particular professions.

4. Beneficial, to give relief in case of death or accidents, as Burial Societies, &c.

5. Dogmatic, to advance some dogma, principle or practice, as Sons of Temperance, &c.

6. Communal, which seek to change the order of Society, as Internationals, &c.

7. Economic, as Sovereigns of Industry, Grangers, &c.

It is a current remark that the interests of labor and capital are identical. The fact is that they may or may not be so.— They are often the very reverse. Capital wishes to have production made cheap and markets high, so that profits may be large or rivals undersold. Labor wants wages high, so that the producer may be better off.

It is obvious that such orders as Masons and Odd Fellows have only a remote influence in harmonizing labor and capital. They are noble institutions, cultivating brotherhood, upholding the manhood of all their members, encouraging morality, and most efficient agencies in sustaining civil and religious liberty, but their scope is not the harmonizing of industrial interests.

Trade societies have certain modes of operation, as : First, restraining production, to the injury of society. Second, compelling the payment of wages which may be just or otherwise, and aiding in controversies which are usually harmful both to employers and employees. Trade unions do not contemplate a change of the relation of labor and capital. They only desire to secure to labor greater rewards.

Beneficial Societies accept social evils as *inevitable* and seek to ameliorate them. They do much good, sometimes harm and are not calculated to eradicate social evils.

Dogmatic Societies seek to change ideas, and their results may be good or bad according to circumstances. So far as they advance truth they are good but the cure of social evils is the secondary anticipated effect of their efforts.

Communal Societies seek to change social order. They see clearly the evils of present arrangements, but their schemes are usually hypothetical, and it is not certain what harms would result from some of the changes they advocate.

Economic Societies may be very advantageous, pecuniarily, to their members by cheapening the cost of living or of business. The feature they most need is the social safety valve of co-operative production and sustaining industrial colonial emigration.

The Roman church has encouraged Beneficial societies controlled by the priesthood but has always bitterly opposed those secret beneficial societies whose basis has been the *equality of men, the protection of personal rights, and absolute religious toleration*.

Masonry through Washington and the other illustrious fathers of American independence, impressed upon American institutions the equality of men, the sanctity of personal rights and absolute religious toleration, and unless Rome has changed she must be hostile to these features.

38

Whether Masonry has been in particular instances perverted is not the issue. It was not the particular perversion to which Rome objected, but the radical principles of Masonry, Odd Fellowship and kindred orders, and so long as Roman Bishops swear to prosecute and wage war with all whom they consider Heretics or Scismatics, Infidels or Jews, they cannot be good Freemasons good Odd Fellows, good Knights of Pythias or good members of any of the other thirty secret beneficial orders that there are in this country.

THE POPE AN EXPELLED MASON.

At the semi-annual meeting of the Grand Lodge of Masons, Scottish Rite of the Orient, of Palermo, Italy, on March 7th, 1874, Pope Pius IX was expelled from the order. This expulsion was published in the official Masonic paper at Cologne, Germany, preceeded by the minutes of the Lodge in which he was initiated, as follows :

"A man named Mastai Ferretti, who received the baptism of Free Masonry, and solemnly pledged his love and fellowship, and who afterward was crowned Pope and King, under the title of Pio Nono, has now cursed his former brethren and excommunicated all members of the Order of Free Masons. Therefore, said Mastai Ferretti is herewith, by decree of the Grand Lodge of the Orient, Palermo, expelled from the Order for perjury."

The charges against him were first preferred at his Lodge at Palermo, in 1865, and notification and copy thereof sent to him, with a request to attend the Lodge for the purpose of answering the same. To this he made no reply, and for divers reasons, the charges were not pressed until he urged the Bishops of Brazil to act aggressively towards the Free Masons. Then they were pressed, and after a regular trial, a decree of expulsion was entered and published, the same being signed by Victor Emmanuel, King of Italy, and Grand Master of the Orient of Italy.

Spirit of the Press.

"The Bohemian paper, the *Pekrok*, supports the public schools, and for this "heresy," the priest has launched against it the curse of Rome. He has prohibited any of his flock from reading it, under pain of eternal punishment. He has also commanded them, in the name of the Church, not to buy goods of any one who subscribes to or reads this paper. The. spirit of bigotry and intolerance that animates this Bohemian priest runs through the whole Church, and if other priests of the city have not ere this hurled their anathemas at the press that supports the public schools it is not through any respect for the press or the schools."—*Cleveland Leader.*

"The constitutional provision in this State is similar to that in New York, and the policy of the Roman Church here will not differ materially from that pursued there, The same power guides them both, and shapes their schemes, with marvelous subtlety, to surrounding circumstances. Did the constitution of New York check them? Not a bit of it. There first move was an attempt to bring their Brooklyn Orphan Asylum under the provisions of the common school fund, while yet retaining absolute control of it. They were fought by the School Trustees, and they (the Roman Catholics) *won their case in the City Courts*, the Constitution to the contrary notwithstanding. The New York common school system owes its protection from this entering wedge only to the fact of having on the bench of its Supreme Court two able Judges, not under the control of the Pope. They overruled the decision of the City Courts; but one of the Judges dissented, the Constitution to the contrary notwithstanding."—*Cincinnati Times*.

"The State rests on the intelligence of its people, and it does well to provide for their education. What it does in this respect should be done for all. The schools should be open to all without regard to their religious belief, and should interfere in no way with the faith or worship of those who enjoy their benefits. They cannot secure those benefits equally to all and serve their full purpose if religious sects, as such, are permitted to control them in any degree. They are at liberty to have schools of their own, and support them from their own means and manage them in their own way, but they should not be allowed to interfere with those of the State which are intended solely for secular instruction and cannot deal practically or beneficially with any other kind. Freedom of religion from State control, freedom of the State from ecclesiastical control and the maintenance of public education for the equal benefit of all, are principles for which all American citizens should stand firm and resolute."—*Boston Globe*.

"The plan of 'Confessional teachings' in the public schools has been tried for years in Prussia, and it was the *abuse of this system by the Catholics* that led to the present conflict between the Roman hierarchy and the State. The custom in Prussia has been to have instruction given in the public schools once or twice a week, in the articles of religion as set forth in the *Confessions* of the Protestant, Roman Catholic and Jewish communions.

" This is the system which Catholics are now seeking to introduce into the common schools of the United States."—*N. Y. Observer.*

" Our excellent Board of Education may see in these signs that the opinion of the American people is that the public school system is *secular*, and no religious body, Protestant or Romanist, may have anything to do with it."—*Christian Advocate.*

"The Roman priesthood, who have now assumed the office of dictator to the Democratic party, do not propose to wait for a legal division of the school fund by constitutional amendment and an act of the Legislature ; they have a much shorter method, which they have already carried out to some extent in some localities, and which they are pushing in all the large cities— namely, to have the School Board take the Roman Church schools into the public pay, while the Church as before appoints the teachers, and they direct the religious services of the schools. In short, the Roman parochial schools, just as they are, are to be supported out of the school fund. They are to be nominally under the control of the School Board, and that board shall go through the form of appointing the teachers nominated to it by the Church."—*Cincinatti Gazette.*

" They must remember, first of all, that after we have given the priests the control of Catholic schools, we shall have only given them a part of what they conceive to be their due. They hold themselves entitled as of right, and solemnly proclaim it, to the control of the education of children of all denominations in every country. Their willingness now to share it with the Protestants in this country is simply a concession to the force of circumstances, which in no way releases them from the obligation of extending the limits of their jurisdiction by every means in their power ; and it behooves those who negotiate with either

Cardinal, archbishop or vicar-general to remember that they negotiate with a 'person who cannot bind himself on subjects of this sort by human conventions. A secret order from Rome may any day relieve him from any stipulation whatever which may seem prejudicial to the interests of the church.

" In the second place, it is folly to suppose that after the Catholics have been allowed to withdraw their share of the school tax from the common fund, or—which is the same thing—been allowed to place their own schools under the Board of Education, other denominations will remain satisfied with the present system ; all religious denominations would like to educate their own children in their own way if they could get the State to raise funds for them by taxation. Episcopalians and Methodists and Baptists support the common schools, not as a perfect system, but as the best attainable system ; but a large part of its efficiency and the whole of its justice would be gone if it was modified to meet the requirements of one religious sect. Moreover—and here is a consideration which the people of this country must face sooner or later, and they may as well begin to face it now—the education given or superintended by Catholic priests is a bad education ; indeed, for political purposes, worse than none. It unfits children for the citizenship of free States. If extended widely enough, it would ruin this Government. It has been tried for ages in various countries, and has in all worked unutterable mischief, and destroyed the sources of national greatness by killing the sincerity, the truthfulness, the courage and high-mindedness on which national greatness is based.— The thoughtful and patriotic men of all Catholic countries are to-day getting rid of it as a national curse. And it would be an astounding spectacle if, after the priests had been excluded from the work of public instruction in France, Spain, Italy and Bavaria, they were to be allowed to carry it on here with taxes voted by American citizens. Compromise with these men has, in short, never succeeeded, and never will. The only thing that does succeed with them is their rigorous subjection to the common law."—*N. Y. Nation.*

The Roman Catholic Church is more thoroughly organized than the Methodist Church, the Presbyterian Church or any other Christian sect. It has among its adherents, as Paganism has, as Mohammedanism has, and as every other religion has, many persons of intelligence, of devoted piety, and of the most self-sacrificing, untiring benevolence. By its wealth, its numbers, its laborous priesthood, its many orders of monks and nuns, its compact organization, its thorough drill, its exceeding craft, and its grasping ambition, the Roman Church is stronger than any other Christian sect; and when the Bishops and Jesuit leaders array it against civil and religious liberty, against the rights of the State, against Public Schools, against the Bible, and against the public money, the duty not only of all Protestants, but of all true men who are Roman Catholics, is to oppose it.

"We stand by free education, our public school system, the taxation of all for its support, and no division of the school fund.—*Ohio Republican Platform* 1875.

"The Democratic Conservatives of Ohio forced to speak, pronounced against Sectarian Control. Then it confesses there is danger. From whom? Undeniably from the Roman Church. But that church works through parties.

"Why now for the first time do political party platforms (of Ohio and California) declare that the unsectarian school system must be maintained? Has the Presbyterian or Methodist or Baptist or Episcopal or Unitarian or Congregational sect, or any sect known as Protestant attacked it? Have the Israelites, or those who own no sectarian Christian name, assailed it? But there is confessedly an assault upon the schools. There is a strong and crafty effort to make them sectarian. It is so powerful and pronounced that the party conventions begin to condemn it, and the whole country knows which sect is plotting the overthrow of unsectarian schools, for it boldly avows its design."—*Harpers' Weekly.*

"But the liberals claim and rightly claim that, from its very nature, the public school system is restricted, that it cannot and does not profess to conduce to every element of an education in the broadest sense. It attempts only to contribute a part of what belongs to the true education. Precisely at this point the secularists take strong exception to the reasoning of the sectarians. They are unable to see why an instrumentality which proposes to give but a part of the whole that is demanded by an education in its highest sense, and which from its nature cannot give more, should be condemned or regarded as dangerous. They deem it to be a mere assumption of the sectarian educationists that a child is exposed to some spiritual danger because during the hours in which he is taught reading, ciphering and geography he does not also learn the Scriptures or the catechism. Is it equally necessary to mix in religious instruction when a boy learns to plow, to mow and to turn the grindstone? Why not? We should all agree that sound physical health demands a variety of food; that all meat and no bread is physically dangerous. But shall we condemn the butcher because he does not furnish bread as well as meat?"—*Independent.*

Sectarian Appropriations.

We find the following in the Baltimore Sun :

The opposition to sectarian appropriations in Baltimore has taken the form of a bill for injunction, filed by several leading taxpayers, to prevent the City Register from paying over to certain institutions therein named the amounts appropriated to them respectively, on the ground that the Charter of the city does not authorize appropriations to private charities. Not all of the institutions named in the bill of complaint are under sectarian control, and of some of them some of the complainants are trustees, which shows that whatever the ulterior motivo there is, at least, an honest purpose to cut off all Sectarian Institutions from the benefits which they have hitherto de-derived from annual appropriations made in their behalf by the Mayor and City Council.

This is but the beginning of what must ultimately grow into a subject of national importance, and if successful before the courts will be followed, no doubt, by the more important movement of compeling the assessment of ecclesiastical property for taxes.

Although the amount drawn out of the treasuries of the various States and municipalities to support Sectarian Institutions under the guise of charity is very large, yet it is insignificant compared to the amount annually bestowed upon religious establishments in the shape of taxes ; and we must say that we think the bill filed for injunction takes hold of the weakest feature of the real case of the People vs. the Religious Establishment, when it simply asks to prevent the payment of money to charities, for it is as charities, and as reformatory institutions beneficial to the public, that they ostensibly appeal for public support, and not sectarian institutions, whereas the churches demand exemption from taxation because they are churches.

There is no denying that some of the foundling and orphan asylums, and industrial schools and homes for the indigent, do perform work which the community needs to have performed and ought to provide for; thus exercising certain civic functions for which they claim recognition; but the churches are devoted exclusively to religious instruction, each according to the faith of its sect, and the constitutions of all the States and of the United States expressly prohibit church establishments. The Maryland declaration of rights declares in Article 36 that "all persons are equally entitled to protection in their religious liberty; nor ought any person be compelled to frequent or maintain, *or contribute unless on contract*, to maintain any place of worship or any ministry," and yet we have the authority of the Appeal Tax Court, as recited by a member of the City Council that the exempted church property of Baltimore city is valued at from $65,000,000 to $70,000,000. The latter sum at the current rate of taxation, would pay nearly $1,500,000 annually into the treasury of the city, which is not far from one-half of the annual expenses proper of maintaining the City government. Thus contrary to the provisions of the constitution of the State, the people of Baltimore are compelled to contribute nearly a million and half dollars a year to maintain a ministry and places of public worship, not far from the amount they pay to support their civil government. If the ecclesiastical property were all assessed and taxed as other property is, the tax bills of the people need only be one-half of what they now are. The man whose tax bill is one hundred dollars could then get off with fifty; and it is an outrage on the constitution as well as upon the principles of civil liberty, to compel a man who does not belong to any sect to pay annually a large sum of money for the support of all, or to compel the member of one congregation, who thinks his route to Heaven the only safe and sure one, to help support another, whose teachings wound his conscience.

It is the poor, laboring man after all, who is the greatest sufferer. He may worship in a church or chapel which costs $5,000 or $10,000 and to get it exempted from taxation he accepts a principle of universal exemption which makes him contribute to pay, not his proportion of the assessment on $5,000 or $10,000, but on $70,000,000. To keep from paying $100 taxes on his own little church, he has to help pay $1,500,000 on all the vast and expensive churches. There are churches enjoying large incomes from rented property, and priests and parsons living in palaces which pay no taxes.

It seems to us that there is a big hole in this Baltimore bill for injunction, which needs to be filled with a call on the city for an account of exemptions, and restraint of all tax collections till they are included in the list, according to the true spirit and letter of the constitution of the State.— *Washington, (D. C.) Daily Critic.*

----------◆----------

THE TAXATION OF CHURCH PROPERTY.

The constitutions of the several states of the Union, considered in relation to the manner in which they deal with the question of taxing church property, may be arranged into five classes. In the first class, embracing the States of California, Connecticut, Delaware, Georgia, Iowa, Kentucky, Maine, Maryland, Massachusetts, Michigan, Nebraska, New Hampshire, New Jersey, New York, Rhode Island and Vermont—sixteen states in all—there are no constitutional provisions on the subject. The question of taxing or exempting church property in these states, not being determined by their fundamental law, is left to the discretion of their respective legislatures in the general exercise of the taxing power. As a matter of fact, we believe that exemption by legislative statute is the rule adopted in all or nearly all of these states. In the states of Florida, Illinois, Indiana, Louisiana, Nevada, North Carolina, Ohio, Oregon, Pennsylvania, South Carolina, Tennessee, Texas, Virginia and Wisconsin—fifteen States in all—the question is expressly remitted to the discretion of their several legislatures. In the third class, embracing the State of Minnesota, it is made the duty of the legislature, by positive command, to exempt church property from all taxation. In the fourth class, embracing the states of Arkansas and Kansas, the legislature is expresly forbidden to impose any tax on church property.

Three states—Alabama, Mississippi and Missouri—constituting the fifth and last class, require church property to be taxed in common with all other property, and thus in effect forbid any exemption in its favor. The constitution of Alabama says: "The property of corporations, now existing or hereafter created, shall forever be subject to taxation, the same as the property of Individuals, except corporations for educational and charitable purposes." The exception clearly does not include religious corporations. The constitution of Mississippi says : " Taxation shall be equal and uniform throughout the state. All property shall be taxed in proportion to its value, to be ascertained as directed by law." The constitution of Missouri says : " No property, real or personal, shall be exempted from taxation, except such as may be used exclusively for public schools and such as may belong to the United States, to this state, to counties, or to municipal corporations within this state." These constitutional provisions exclude church property from any tax exemption.

We have, then, as the result, thirty-one states whose constitutions, either expressly or impliedly, leave the question of taxation in respect to church property to the discretion of their legislatures; one state that imposes upon its legislature the duty of exempting such property; two states that formally deny to their legislatures the right of taxing church property; and three states whose constitutions forbid any tax exemption in favor of churches. Precisely what is the practice in all these states we do not know; yet in the majority of them, church property pays not a dollar of taxes. The question whether this system of exemption, either by constitutional or legislative authority, shall be continued, has· within the last few years elicited much discussion. The tax burdens of the people have been enormously increased, as a consequence of the late war; and feeling the weight, they naturally inquire whether these burdens are equitably distributed. The statistics as to church property in the several states present a huge mass of corporate property on which no taxes are levied; and the question is whether there is any good reason, especially under our system of government, for extending such a system of favoritism to this species of property.—*Independent*.

The Pope on Civil and Religious Laws.

M. Perin, Professor of Jurisprudence at Louvain, the author of a work entitled "The Laws of Christian Society," has received a letter from the Pope, complimenting him on his defence of the principle that civil ought to agree with religious laws. After remarking that deviations from this rule may be tolerated if circumstances require it, and if the object is to avoid greater evils, but that they cannot be raised to the dignity of rights, the Pope says :

" *Would to God that these truths were understood* by those who boast themselves to be Catholics, although they obstinately adhere to liberty of conscience, liberty of creed, the freedom of the press, and similar kinds of liberty which were established by the revolutionists at the end of the last century, and which the Church has always condemned. Those who adhere to those liberties, not only as far as they may be tolerated, but consider them as rights which must be advocated and defended as necessary to the present state of things and to the march of progress, as if everything opposed to the true religion, everything which attributes self-government to man and frees him from the Divine authority, everything which opens a broad road to all errors and corruption of morals could give the nations prosperity, progress and glory—if these men had not put their own opinions above the teachings of the Church; if, perhaps without knowing it, they had not lent a friendly hand to those who cherish hatred of religious authority and civil authority; if they had not thus divided the united forces of the Catholic family, the daring machinations of disturbers would have been restrained, and we should not have reached a point at which we have to fear the subversion of all order."

MORE OF THE OATH.

A correspondent of the *Non-Conformist* (London) furnishes to that paper an authentic copy of the Cardinal's oath, as furnished to Lord Palmerston in 1850 by the British minister at Turin. The following passage from it will fully explain its scope and spirit:

"I, —— ——, Cardinal of the Holy Roman Church, do promise and swear that, from this time to my life's end, I will be faithful and obedient unto St. Peter, the Holy Apostolic Roman Church, and our most Holy Lord the Pope, and his successors, canonically and lawfully elected; that I will give no advice, consent, or assistance against the Pontifical Majesty and person; that I will never knowingly or advisedly, to their injury or disgrace, make public the counsels intrusted to me by themselves, or by messengers or letters (from them;) also, that I will give them any assistance in retaining, defending, and recovering the Roman Papacy and the regalia of Peter with all my might and endeavor, so far as the rights and privileges of my order will allow it, and will defend against all their honor and state; that I will direct and defend, with due form and honor, the legates and nuncios of the Apostolic See in the territories, churches, monasteries, and other benefices committed to my keeping; that I will cordially co-operate with them, and treat them with honor in their coming, abiding, and returning, and that I will resist unto blood all persons whatsoever who shall attempt anything against them; that I will by every way and by every means strive to preserve, argument, and advance the rights, honors, privileges, the authority of the Holy Roman Bishop our Lord the Pope, and his before-mentioned successors; and that at whatever time any thing shall be decided to their prejudice, which it is out of my power to hinder, as soon as I shall know that any steps or measures have been taken (in the matter,) I will make it known to the same our Lord, or his before-mentioned successors, or to some other person by whose means it may be brought to their knowledge. That I will keep and carry out, and cause others to keep and carry out, the rules of the Holy Father, the decrees, ordinances, dispensations, reservations, provisions, apostolic mandates, and constitutions of the Holy Pontiff Sixtus of happy memory, as to visiting the thresholds of the apostles at certain prescribed times, according to the tenor of that which I have just read through. That I will seek out and oppose, persecute and fight against [Latin—*omni conatu persecuturum et impugnaturum*] heretics, schismatics, against the same our Lord the Pope and his before-mentioned successors, with every possible effort."

NO ATTACK ON RELIGION.

In the preparation of this little manual there has been a wish to avoid all reflections on the doctrines or ceremonies, the dogmas or forms of the Roman Catholic Church. Whether its dogmas are true or false is not within the scope of the present work. Whether it is more truthful or less so than one or other sort of Protestantism, has nothing to do with the inquiry how far the men who control the church organization are friends or foes of entire religious toleration, of freedom of speech and the press, of free public schools, uncontrolled by any religious sect and of the State as independent of any church alliance or control.

All intelligent Protestants will admit that the Roman Catholic Church teaches some truth, and it is not the purpose of this work to determine how much. All liberal minded Protestants will admit that there are many Roman Catholics of exemplary character and lives, honorable, truthful, self-sacrificing and laborious in works of mercy. Whether they are more or less exemplary in their lives has nothing to do with the inquiry whether the great organization to which they belong is directed by men whose sympathies and purposes are opposed to religious toleration, and who would, if they could, crush free institutions.

There is no question whether there are Roman Catholics who are good people, but the question is whether the army to which they belong is to be hurled against the public schools and the constitutional guarantees of civil and religious liberty. In considering this last we do not charge that all the tricks of the Ring are suggested or sanctioned by Roman Catholic Bishops or Jesuits. They use the Ring. They give it a power it would not otherwise possess. We oppose the practices of the Ring and the designs of Rome. *The author of this little book is not a member of any political party, and would be a democrat if democracy was not unworthy of the name.*

* * * * *

NO ATTACK ON RACE OR NATIVITY.

Men of German and Irish, of Spanish and Italian blood have been as devoted friends of free institutions as any others. They have freely shed their blood for civil and religious liberty.—They are all welcome to the ranks of the army rallying round the public schools and constitutional rights. They have a common interest in transmitting to posterity all the liberties

54

that they enjoy. They have a common interest in putting an
end to Ring rule, and the co-operation of all good men is desired.
Let none then utter the lie that the defence of free institutions
is coupled with the ostracising of men on account of birthplace.
If a man is a true man, if he is opposed to all encroachments
on entire religious toleration, if he is opposed to all assaults on
or undermining of our public school system, if he is opposed to
all support of sectarianism by the use of public money, if he is
opposed to the corruption and dishonesty of ring rule, then the
friends of reform have not a thought of rejecting his fellowship.

THINGS THAT MUST BE CHANGED.

The purchase of offices by corrupt aspirants whose hirelings
control primary elections.

The multiplication of useless officials to increase partisan
patronage.

The increase of taxes until, in many cases, they are one-third
as much as the net revenues from property.

The neglect of the commercial interests of Baltimore.

The protection and encouragement of favored gambling
houses.

The putting lawyers, cobblers and carpenters in the School
Board to direct the management of schools, about which they
are profoundly ignorant.

The releasing bummers from jail weekly, so that they may be immediately re-arrested and re-committed at the expense of the city, to the great profit of police magistrates.

The bounty paid for compelling prisoners to ship on fishing vessels.

The constant increase of city expenditures and city debt.

The giving away of public money to further private or sectarian projects.

The periodical black-mail of disreputable houses.

The collection of over $600,000 taxes unjustly to make good the deficit of property exempt from taxation.

The neglect of any plan for excluding filth from the Basin by closing the upper end of private sewers.

The do-nothing policy in relation to public improvements.

The making the public yard a political machine for the support of partisan bummers.

The bribery to have railroad tracks kept in or removed from certain streets.

The bribery to effect a reduction of the park tax on city passenger railroads.

The anticipated bribery to secure a renewal of the contract with the gas company.

The anticipated bribery to secure the abolition of the commutation on Baltimore and Ohio Railroad, so that it may be entirely free from taxes of any kind.

The anticipated bribery to secure the sale of the interest of the city in Western Maryland Railroad for less than half what it is worth.

The anticipated bribery to secure the loan of another million dollars to the suspended Valley Railroad, of which P. P. Pendleton is president.

No union of the highest Republican official with a candidate of the ring to put bogus candidates forward.

No ten thousand fraudulent names on the registry lists.

No fifty thousand dollars fraud in the purchase of ground and the erection of the House of Correction.

CAUTIONS.

Those who rally to defend free institutions, justice and equal rights, must not imagine that their victory will be an easy one. They will be opposed by numbers, by sectarian craft, and by all the arts of unscrupulous ring politicians. They should expect that in some localities ignorant majorities may be misled to the support of injustice, monopolies and class privileges.— They should expect that often the clear will of intelligent majorities will be over-ridden for a time by ballot-box stuffing, by

57

fraudulent votes of substitutes or repeaters, and by dishonest election returns. That truth and right, justice and liberty will ultimately triumph there is no doubt, but there may be men who join a good cause and who are unduly depressed because fraud snatches from them the success achieved or victory does not at once crown their efforts. To such men a few words of caution may not be improper.

If you suppose the struggle is a mere contest for the spoils of office, you are not needed in the army of liberty. If you are governed by selfish desire to get office, you are at heart as rotten as the ring politicians you oppose. If you suppose that the defense of civil and religious liberty *for all*, free public unsectarian schools *for all*, and just taxation *for all* involves rancor, bitterness, hate or wrong to men because they were not born on American soil, or because they belong to the Roman Catholic Church you do not harmonize with the great American ideas upon which free institutions must be upheld.

If you have even shed your blood for American institutions, what more have you done than thousands of heroic Irishmen and Germans? Are you a truer friend of civil and religious liberty than Lafayette was, than Daniel O'Connell was, or than tens of thousands of men in all countries are the wide world over?

Be true to yourself and your country. Be rancorous to none. Be undaunted by all reverses. Be free from mean and petty selfishness, and you will be one of the saviours of your country, and a blessing to your children, and the children of those who now oppose you. Have no hate to any men of any sect or party, but trust only those candidates for office whom you believe to be trustworthy. Oppose to the utmost all sectarian schemes that are intollerant and inimical to civil and religious liberty; but if a man is a true man, whose principles are right, and his heart right, give him the justice and honor that he deserves wherever you find him.

ALAS FOR TAX PAYERS.

A number of the most reliable real estate brokers in this city have been asked how they think Ring Rule is afflicting property in Baltimore, and the following are some of their replies :

"The average net profit on real estate is a little less than six per cent. on the gross rents or not much over 3.46 per cent. on the assessment."

"In one case, illustrating many, the *City taxes alone* are over 36 per cent. on the net receipts after deducting expenses, or over 23 per cent. on gross rents."

"One piece of property in Baltimore county is valued by its owner at $65,000, but it is assessed at $11,995, and its County tax is $61,45. If it was in Baltimore city it would be assessed at its full value and pay a City tax of $117."

"I am unable to sell for $9000 a piece of property that I own but the assessment of that property is $12,000 on which I pay taxes."

"There are over five thousand houses standing tenantless at this time."

" When last season one of our shrewdest real estate men was required to testify in a case at Annapolis, he swore that since 1871 all property in Baltimore, except on Baltimore street, between Gay and Eutaw streets, and contiguous to the approaches to Druid Hill Park, had declined in value from 33 to 50 per cent."

"In the City Council recently a member declared that in a number of streets of south Baltimore property was not worth as much as it was 14 years ago."

"The numerous Trustees' sales on almost every day show that really many people cannot afford to hold real estate."

"Houses in many cases do not bring one-third or one-half of their actual cost, yet often they are assessed so high that they would not sell for one-half as much."

"A piece of property assessed at $13,000 sold in 1873 for $5,000, but the owner continues to pay taxes on $13,000."

" A piece of property assessed at $25,000 has just been sold for $15,000, which is considered all that it is worth."

"There are no exceptions to the rule that taxes are going up and few exceptions to the fact that rents on all business property are going down."

"I have a house that is assessed for $4,288 and I dare any man living to pay me $2,600 for it. It still goes on paying taxes on $4,288."

" Mr. W—— offered a check for $16,000 for a house some time ago. He has just bought the house for $9,000."

"Houses on St. Paul street that it cost $10,000 to build are not worth $3,000."

"Houses that cost $25,000 are not yielding rents equal to six per cent. on half that amount."

"An up-town block of buildings were assessed for $25,00 each, but one of the houses has just been sold for $1,150 and another for $1,050."

"Property generally is not selling for what it was in 1867."

"I own a house that is assessed at $33,500; but I cannot get it sold for $18,000. As I pay taxes on $33,500 I asked the Appeal Tax Court to reduce the amount; but they said they had no power to do so."

"The rate of taxation is going upward rapidly, and the value of property is going down steadily. I don't think it can be stopped except by an entire overturning of the present city government."

"If the accounts of the City could be examined the most tremendous frauds would be discovered; but no person is allowed to make such an examination."

"Browning was used as a scape-goat, but he did not get all the tricks."

WHAT DOES HE MEAN.

The imported editor of the *Catholic Mirror* is very bitter at somebody. He says:

"Yet it appears that there are traitors in our midst, poor, peddling traitors, who conspire to assail and destroy that much envied *Constitution*," [which he says is the Declaration of Independence.] "Poor" traitors must mean some mendicant order. "Peddling" traitors, those who are trying to barter political influence for the control of the "godless" public

61

schools which they hate. He says, those "poor," "peddling" traitors "hold their conclaves in silence and in secrecy." Is that what is called in a "retreat." They endeavor to rally bigotry and ignorance around them for their baleful work." Who is it that rallies the ignorant and the bigoted to war on religious toleration and on the public schools? This truculent writer on what he don't understand says, "under that covenant assured to the people of this republic, the right to worship God as each man pleased, is affirmed the greatest doctrine that could contribute and insure peace amongst our people." Don't he know that the right of any man to be a heretic, or schismatic or any thing but a Roman Catholic is what the Roman Catholic Church always has denied, and the Roman Pope and Bishops now deny. He can find where they assert that a man has a right to be a Roman Catholic, which no one denies; but let him show where his church and his bishops have not been bitterly opposed to toleration of other religions. He says:

"The world had grown tired of the compulsory efforts of the bigot, the worst bigot, the worst tyrant of all to trample the soul and abrogate, the God born right of religious liberty.

It had grown tired of the reeking scaffold, and the hideous torture, and the horrible scenes of roasting at the stake and crushing at the wheel." Who were the bigots who tried to trample on the soul and tried to abrogate the God born right of religious liberty? Who used the dungeon, the rack, the torture chamber, the auto-de-fe?

He says "The American Republic at its dawn declared that no man's pursuit of happiness should be implied by reason of his holding any dogma of belief, following any form of worship or promulgating any tenets that he thought fit and proper. Mankind everywhere hailed the boon with praise and rapture, and its idea, the idea of leaving the sovl untrammelled as the Creator had left it, came with a freshness and beauty all its own upon the heart of civilization." It certainly did not come from the Roman Catholic Church which had for more than a thousand years been claiming exactly the reverse. This defender of toleration don't perhaps know that Archbishop Bayley says they "must return to the old paths.". This gushing writer may sincerely love liberty and toleration. He certainly does not show that he knows either what the friends of public schools and civil and religious liberty propose nor what his own Church and its Bishops claim

Of the former he says "Do they think that they will raise any agitation amongst the Catholics, whom they menace?"

We would reply that they don't think so, and don't menace anybody, but this Roman Candle asks the question : "Do they think that they will raise any agitation amongst the Catholics, whom they menace?" And he forthwith replies : To this latter question we can give answer, "They will not." "Do they think, &c.," he asks, and he answers it, "They will not."

A writer in this style must not be held to rigid rules of logic and common sense.

We are glad that he is a friend of religious toleration, and regret that he does not know more of what he is writing about.

SELFISHNESS.

The chief danger to every organization honestly seeking political reform is not from the opposition of external enemies; but from bad elements in or injudicious measures by the organization itself.

Even among the twelve disciples of Jesus there was a Judas, and there are in most political associations some men who for a little money or even the promise of appointments will betray the cause to enable its enemies to counteract and defeat its efforts, or by the formenting of feuds destroy its force. To guard as far as possible against such treachery, certain principles will be found advantageous.

Let the organization be thorough, complete, just and truly American, by its reliance on popular will.

Let each branch be complete and strict in its organization Let its officers be men who are known to be devoted to principle, judicious and unflinching. Let the central body be composed of men nominated by the best men of the branch, and approved by a decided majority of the members of the branch.

Let the members of the central body not be in as great haste to nominate somebody for public office as to build up the organization and disseminate its principles.

Let them be strictly just in their control, but inflexible in maintaining the unity of the organization by stamping out of it any man or set of men who upon fair trial are found to be unworthy. Some men would not willingly betray the cause for their own pecuniary advantage, but may imperil it by petty egotism aspiring to positions in the organization as stepping stones to public office in the future, or by selfish stupidity urging particular plans that they originate or by feuds growing out of nasty little jealousies.

There is always danger that mean rivalries for small honors may beget distrust, divisions, forgetfulness of the great objects to be achieved, and consequent in harmony and weakness. To guard against these things keeping constantly in view the ends to be attained and the principles to be upheld and selecting carefully the men to control the branch societies, and the whole grand movement are of the utmost importance.

The great majority of members in a reform association will be disinterested, patriotic men and they should frown down Judases, mischief makers, and pretensious asses who are inspired by selfishness and who in many cases are neither fitted by nature nor education for the station they desire.

In my opinion it would be wise for every member of the organization to make up his mind individually that he will not support for ANY ELECTIVE OFFICE any member of the organization, but when the reform is carried he will do his utmost to have members of the reform organization *appointed* in public office.

Adopt this policy and the reform will not be broken up by feuds or selfish schemes; but will devote itself to selecting candidates who can be trusted and will be fit. If the reform is carried there will be enough appointments to be given out to supply every good man who wishes a public position. This will secure harmony, and in my opinion is the true policy, while reform is in its infancy, and its opponents have great facilities for corruption.

A FINAL APPEAL.

Baltimore needs above all else deliverance from a horde of corrupt demagogues, led on by the Court House Ring. One class of men desire such deliverance because the Ring panders to designs on civil and religious liberty; another class want it because Ring jobbery bankrupts the City Treasury and enormously increases taxes; a third class wishes it because primary elections have been made infamously corrupt, and a fourth class because under Ring rule the best men in the Democratic party or in the community have not the slightest influence in the management of public affairs. One man may suppose that if good men are placed in office instead of political schemers, the evils wou'd be corrected; another may believe that guarding the public schools is more important than any other duty, and a third may feel that debt and taxes, corrupt jobbery and public plunder are the greatest blights on the prosperity of Baltimore.

Honest men may differ in their estimate of the comparative harm done in one way or another by the Court House Ring, but they will all see that the Ring must be beaten at the polls, and thus driven from the positions they prostitute before any reform can be secured.

Let all, then, unite heartily in working for the overthrow of Ring rule.

The hounds who bark at their masters' order may swear that opposition to the Ring is Know-Nothingism, or Nativism, or Anti-Catholicism, or Communism, or Anti-Democracy, or Anti-Americanism, but the fact is that it has one ruling thought, "opposition to the Court House Ring and its practices," and one fixed purpose—

THE DEFEAT OF THE RING.

www.ingramcontent.com/pod-product-compliance
Lightning Source LLC
Chambersburg PA
CBHW021629270326
41931CB00008B/940